AFRICA

Written by Rob Colson
Illustrated by Josy Bloggs

Published in 2025 by Enslow Publishing, LLC
2544 Clinton Street
Buffalo, NY 14224

First published in Great Britain in 2023
by Hodder & Stoughton

Copyright © Hodder & Stoughton Limited, 2023

Series Editor: Amy Pimperton
Editor: Nicola Hodgson
Series Designer: Ed Simkins
Illustrator: Josy Bloggs
Map illustrator: Amy Zhing

All rights reserved. No part of this book may be reproduced in any form without permission in writing from the publisher, except by a reviewer.

Manufactured in the United States of America

CPSIA compliance information: Batch #CSENS25: For further information contact Enslow Publishing LLC, New York, New York at 1-800-398-2504.

Please visit our website, www.enslowpublishing.com. For a free color catalog of all our high-quality books, call toll free 1-800-398-2504 or fax 1-877-980-4454.

Cataloging-in-Publication Data

Names: Colson, Rob, author. | Bloggs, Josy, illustrator.
Title: Africa / by Rob Colson, illustrated by Josy Bloggs.
Description: Buffalo, NY : Enslow Publishing, 2025. | Series: Continents uncovered | Includes glossary and index.
Identifiers: ISBN 9781978539044 (pbk.) | ISBN 9781978539051 (library bound) | ISBN 9781978539068 (ebook)
Subjects: LCSH: Africa--Juvenile literature.
Classification: LCC DT3.C657 2025 | DDC 960--dc23

We recommend adult supervision at all times while doing the activities in this book. Always be aware that craft materials may contain allergens, so check the packaging for allergens if there is a risk of an allergic reaction. Anyone with a known allergy must avoid these.

- Wear an apron and cover surfaces.
- Tie back long hair.
- Ask an adult for help with cutting and glueing.
- Check materials for allergens.

Find us on

CONTENTS

WHERE IN THE WORLD? 4

NORTHERN AFRICA 6

SAHARA DESERT 8

CENTRAL AFRICA 10

CONGO RAINFOREST 12

RIFT VALLEY LAKES.............................14

MOUNT KILIMANJARO 16

SERENGETI NATIONAL PARK 18

SOUTHERN AFRICA 20

MADAGASCAR...22

OKAVANGO DELTA.................................24

PEOPLE AND PLACES 26

QUIZ AND GLOSSARY 30

INDEX...32

WHERE IN THE WORLD?

Africa is the second-largest continent in the world after Asia, by both size and human population. The continent straddles the equator. It is connected to Asia in the northeast by a narrow strip of land between Egypt and the Sinai Peninsula. It is separated from Europe in the northwest by the Strait of Gibraltar, which is just 7.5 miles (12 kilometers) wide at its narrowest point.

POLITICAL MAP   PHYSICAL MAP

MAKING MAPS

Mapmakers create maps that show many different types of information. Political maps show human features, such as countries, as seen on the map to the far left. Physical maps highlight the geographical features of a region, such as the height of the land above sea level. The physical map of Africa to the left shows low areas in green and high ground in orange.

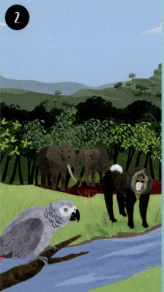

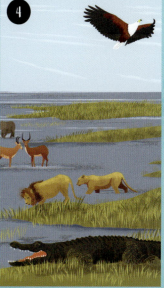

HABITATS

A habitat is an area that is home to a particular group of plants and animals. The continent of Africa contains a huge range of habitats. Hot deserts, such as the Sahara (1) are home to only a few plants and animals that are able to survive the harsh conditions. By contrast, lush rainforests, such as the Congo (2), abound with a rich variety of life. Herds of large animals graze the open grasslands of the Serengeti National Park (3), while many creatures head for the Okavango Delta (4) when it floods each year.

FACTS

- Area: 11.7 million square miles (30.4 million sq km)
- Major rivers: Nile, Congo, Niger, Zambezi, Orange
- Highest peak: Mount Kilimanjaro, Tanzania, 19,340 feet (5,895 meters)
- Major mountain ranges: Atlas Mountains, Ruwenzori, Ethiopian Highlands (including the Simien Mountains), Drakensberg Mountains

NORTHERN AFRICA

Northern Africa is dominated by the giant Sahara Desert, the largest hot desert in the world. Few creatures can survive in this harsh habitat, but life springs up around isolated oases. The River Nile flows through the east of northern Africa, while the west is dominated by the rugged Atlas Mountains.

HIGHS & LOWS

RECORD HIGH TEMPERATURE: 124.3°F (51.3°C), OUARGLA, ALGERIA

DRIEST PLACE: KUFRA, LIBYA, .03 IN (.75 MM) RAIN PER YEAR

CANARY ISLANDS

ATLAS MOUNTAINS

THE SAHEL

ATLANTIC OCEAN

CAMELS

Dromedary camels are well adapted to life in the African desert. They can go for more than a week without drinking, then gulp down more than 50 gallons (190 l) of water. Camels are domesticated animals, meaning that they have been specially bred by humans. Today, people use dromedary camels for transport and as a source of milk and meat.

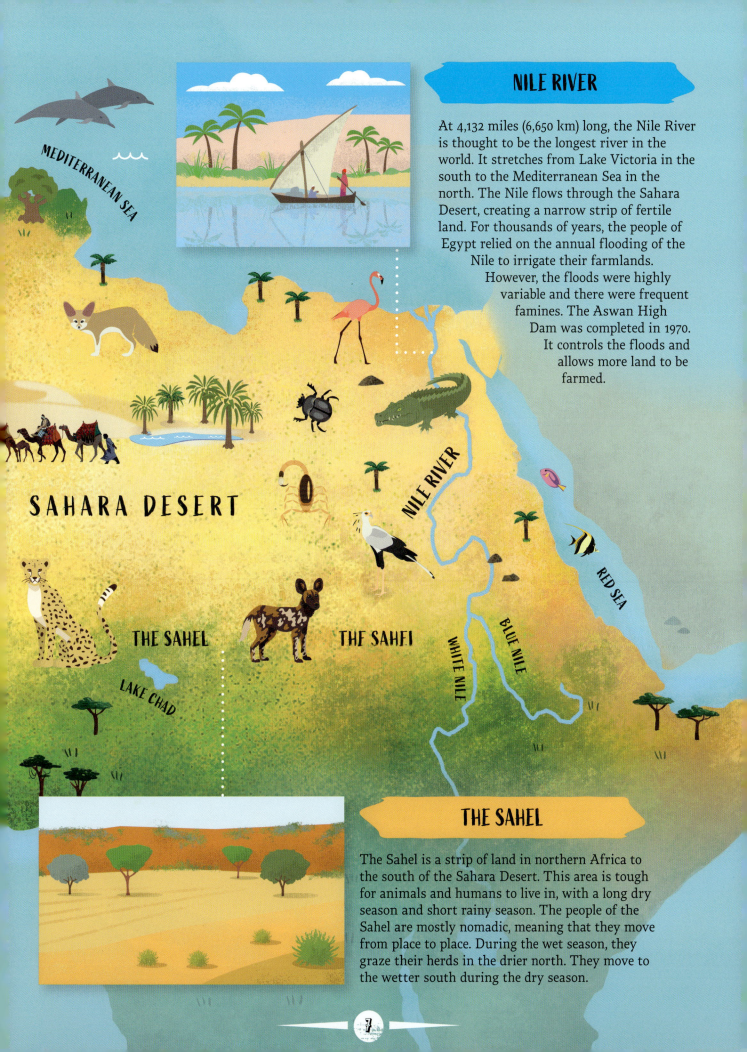

SAHARA DESERT

The Sahara is the largest hot desert in the world, covering most of northern Africa. It stretches 2,983 miles (4,800 km) from the Red Sea in the east to the Atlantic Ocean in the west. Much of the desert is too dry to support many living things, but life thrives around oases, where natural springs rise to the surface to provide water.

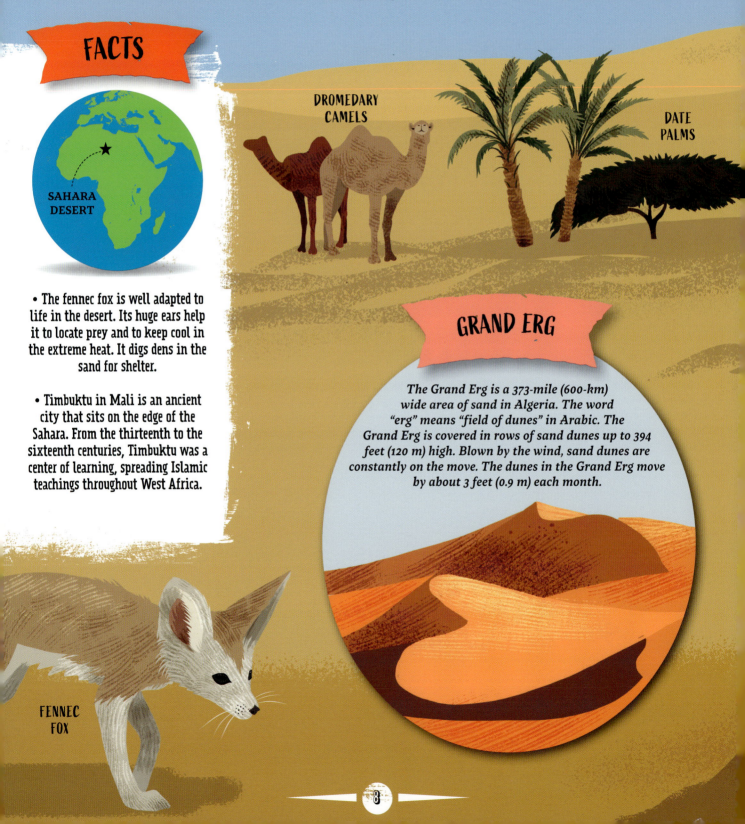

DROMEDARY CAMELS

DATE PALMS

FACTS

SAHARA DESERT

- The fennec fox is well adapted to life in the desert. Its huge ears help it to locate prey and to keep cool in the extreme heat. It digs dens in the sand for shelter.

- Timbuktu in Mali is an ancient city that sits on the edge of the Sahara. From the thirteenth to the sixteenth centuries, Timbuktu was a center of learning, spreading Islamic teachings throughout West Africa.

GRAND ERG

The Grand Erg is a 373-mile (600-km) wide area of sand in Algeria. The word "erg" means "field of dunes" in Arabic. The Grand Erg is covered in rows of sand dunes up to 394 feet (120 m) high. Blown by the wind, sand dunes are constantly on the move. The dunes in the Grand Erg move by about 3 feet (0.9 m) each month.

FENNEC FOX

OSTRICH

SCORPION

ACTIVITY

Moving sand dunes

Create your own sand dunes and watch how they move as you blow on them.

1. Ask an adult to help you cover the bottom of a shallow plastic container or box with a layer of sand.

2. Use a straw to gently blow on the sand to create dunes. Can you make your dunes move from one end of the container to the other?

BIOKO ISLAND

San Antonio de Ureka, on the island of Bioko off the west coast of Africa, is the wettest place on the continent, with more than 394 inches (10,000 mm) of rainfall each year. During the short dry season between November and March, sea turtles, such as green turtles and leatherbacks, haul themselves onto the beaches of Bioko to lay their eggs.

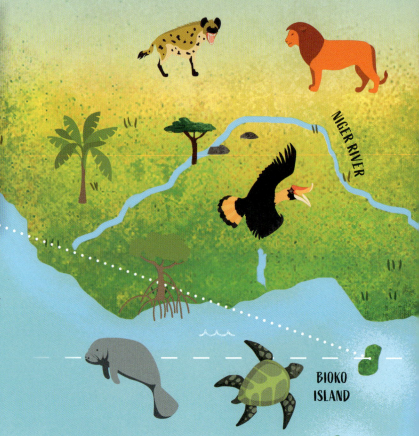

CENTRAL AFRICA

Central Africa straddles the equator. It is hot all year round, and there is plenty of rainfall, leading to dense tropical rainforests in the western half of Central Africa. Farther east, rainfall is seasonal and the landscape is dominated by open grasslands.

ATLANTIC OCEAN

ETHIOPIAN HIGHLANDS

Most of Ethiopia in East Africa is covered by the Ethiopian Highlands, a mix of mountains and high plateaus known as the Roof of Africa. The animals found here include the walia ibex, a goat that lives on narrow mountain ledges, and the mountain nyala, a hardy antelope that lives in alpine forests. Packs of Ethiopian wolves patrol the remote areas, feeding on rodents such as the giant mole rat.

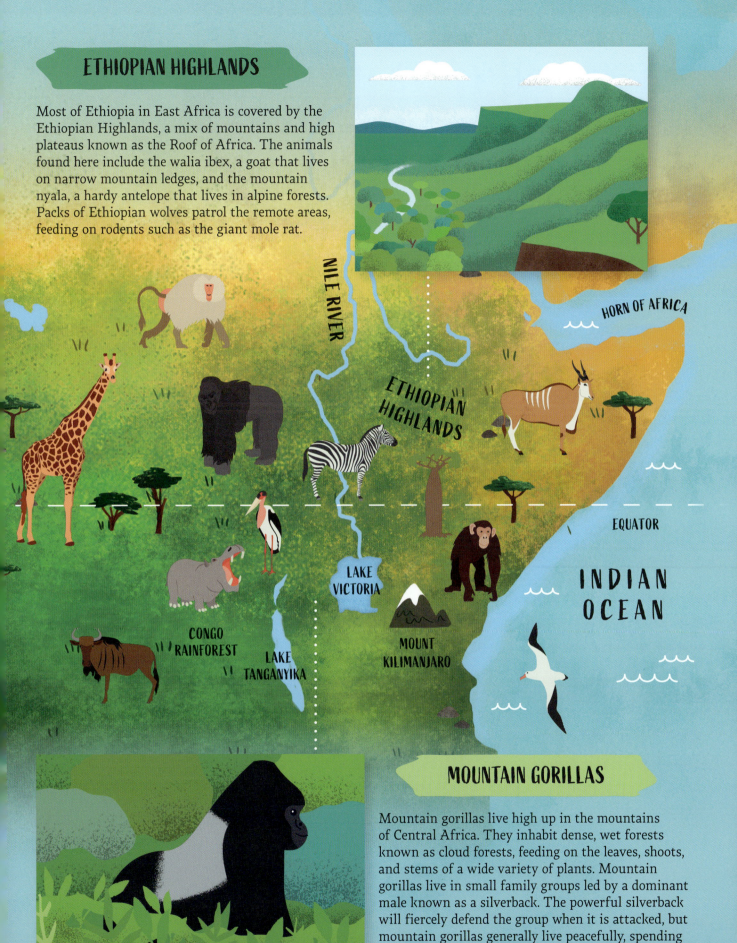

MOUNTAIN GORILLAS

Mountain gorillas live high up in the mountains of Central Africa. They inhabit dense, wet forests known as cloud forests, feeding on the leaves, shoots, and stems of a wide variety of plants. Mountain gorillas live in small family groups led by a dominant male known as a silverback. The powerful silverback will fiercely defend the group when it is attacked, but mountain gorillas generally live peacefully, spending much of the day grooming, eating, or playing.

CONGO RAINFOREST

The Congo Rainforest is the second-largest tropical forest in the world, after the Amazon Rainforest. The forest fans out around the mighty Congo River as it flows toward the Atlantic Ocean. It is home to an amazing range of plants and animals, including three species of great ape: chimpanzees, bonobos, and gorillas.

FACTS

- The African gray parrot lives in dense forest areas. It is a highly intelligent bird, and captive African grays have been taught to speak hundreds of words and even perform simple math.

- The marbled lungfish lives in shallow rivers and lakes. It survives dry seasons by burrowing into the ground and breathing air with its lungs. This eel-like fish can grow more than 6.5 feet (2 m) long.

FOREST ELEPHANTS

MANDRILL

AFRICAN GRAY PARROT

BONOBOS

Along with chimpanzees, bonobos are the closest relatives of human beings. These peace-loving primates are found in the forests south of the Congo River. Bonobos live in groups led by older females. They feed mostly on fruit and band together to hunt monkeys and squirrels.

OKAPI

DWARF CROCODILE

ACTIVITY

Paper parrot

Make a colorful parrot out of a paper plate.

1. With the help of an adult, cut a large paper plate in half. One half will be the head, the other half the body.

2. Use colored markers to paint one half of the head a red beak color and the other half the green face. Glue a googly eye to the head.

3. Ask an adult to help you decorate the body by glueing strips of ribbon or tissue paper to it. These represent the feathers.

4. With an adult's help, staple the two plates together to complete your paper plate parrot.

RIFT VALLEY LAKES

The Rift Valley Lakes are a series of lakes in East Africa, stretching from Ethiopia in the north to Malawi in the south. They include Lake Victoria, the largest lake in Africa. Many birds and mammals gather to feed in the lakes, which are home to hundreds of kinds of fish that are unique to the area.

FACTS

- Hippos live in rivers, lakes, and swamps. They spend the daytime keeping cool in the water, emerging onto land in the evening to graze on the grass.

- The Maasai people graze their cattle on the plains around the Rift Valley Lakes. The traditional Maasai diet includes a drink made by mixing cow's milk with cow's blood.

GREAT WHITE PELICAN

HIPPOS

CICHLIDS

The Rift Valley Lakes are home to a wide variety of cichlids. These colorful fish are most abundant in Lake Malawi, which contains nearly 1,000 different species. Female cichlids are choosy about their mates. Some prefer brightly colored males, while others are attracted to males that can perform gymnastic feats such as swimming in a figure eight.

ACTIVITY

Maasai necklace

Make a necklace like those worn by the Maasai people, who live in this region.

1. With help from an adult, use a pair of scissors to cut out the center of a paper plate, leaving a ring. Cut away a small section of the ring, as shown above. Use a hole punch to punch a hole about 1 inch (2.5 cm) from each end.

2. Cut a length of colored yarn about 12 inches (30 cm) long and tie it to each end of the necklace.

3. Use paint to decorate your necklace. Every Maasai necklace is different, so you can create your own pattern. This one has been painted with alternating stripes.

FLAMINGOS

WATER HYACINTH

MONITOR LIZARD

MOUNT KILIMANJARO

Standing 19,340 feet (5,895 m) tall, Mount Kilimanjaro is the highest mountain in Africa. Although it is just 205 miles (330 km) south of the equator, the mountain is so tall that there is always snow on the summit. As you descend from the peak, you pass through many different habitats, including moorland and rainforest, to reach the hot, grassy plains at the bottom.

FACTS

MOUNT KILIMANJARO

- Olive baboons live in the forests of Kilimanjaro. These noisy monkeys live in groups of 15 to 20 individuals. They communicate using a range of different loud grunts.

- At higher altitudes above the tree line, flowering plants called groundsels are found. The largest of these, the giant groundsel, can grow up to 33 feet (10 m) tall.

GIANT GROUNDSEL

SILVERY-CHEEKED HORNBILL

Silvery-cheeked hornbills are large birds that are found in the forests of Kilimanjaro. They live in pairs of a male and a female. During the breeding season, the female shuts herself into a nest in a tree hollow. The male delivers food to the female while she cares for the chicks. The male will deliver about 24,000 pieces of fruit during the four months that the female is walled in. Once the chicks are ready to fly, the female breaks out of her nest.

BUSH PIG

GREAT BLUE TURACO

OLIVE BABOON

COMMON SLENDER MONGOOSE

ACTIVITY

Bubbling volcano

Kilimanjaro is now dormant, but this fizzing volcano activity shows how it erupted in the past.

1. With the help of an adult, cut a disposable paper cup in half so that it is about 2 inches (5 cm) tall. Wrap modeling clay around it to form a cone shape.

2. Place your volcano on a tray in an open space outside. With the permission and help of an adult, pour a couple of tablespoons of baking soda into it.

3. With an adult's help, in a separate cup, mix vinegar with a couple of drops of red food coloring. Pour the red vinegar over the baking soda and watch what happens!

SERENGETI NATIONAL PARK

Serengeti National Park in Tanzania is home to many of the world's largest land animals. Most of the park is a savanna habitat, with a mix of widely spread trees and grasses. Huge herds of zebra and wildebeest pass through the park every year to graze on the grasslands, hotly pursued by predators, such as lions and hyenas.

FACTS

- Nile crocodiles patrol the Mara River, picking off wildebeest and zebra as they swim across the river.

- A leopard will often drag its prey up a tree following a kill. This allows it to feed in peace without having to worry about rival predators such as lions stealing its meal.

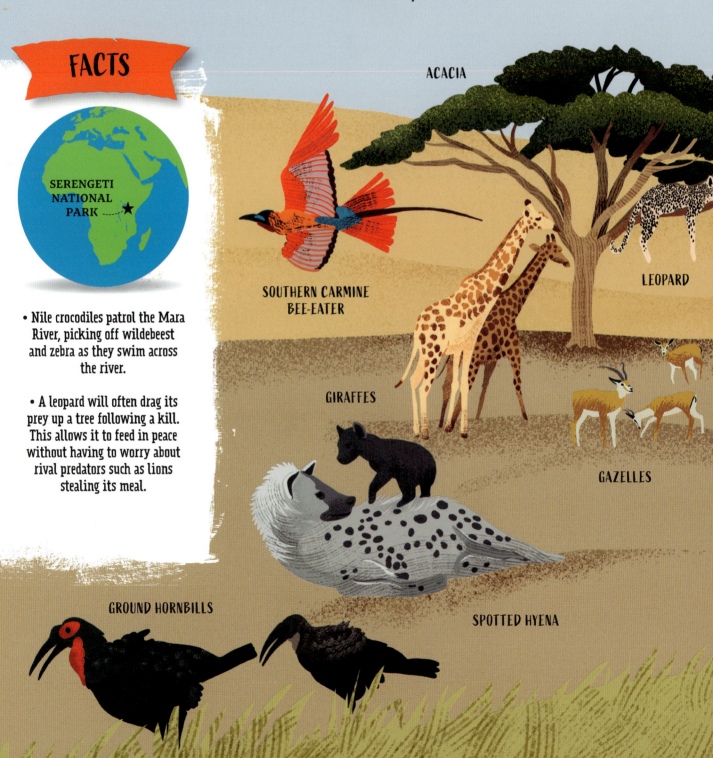

MIGRATION

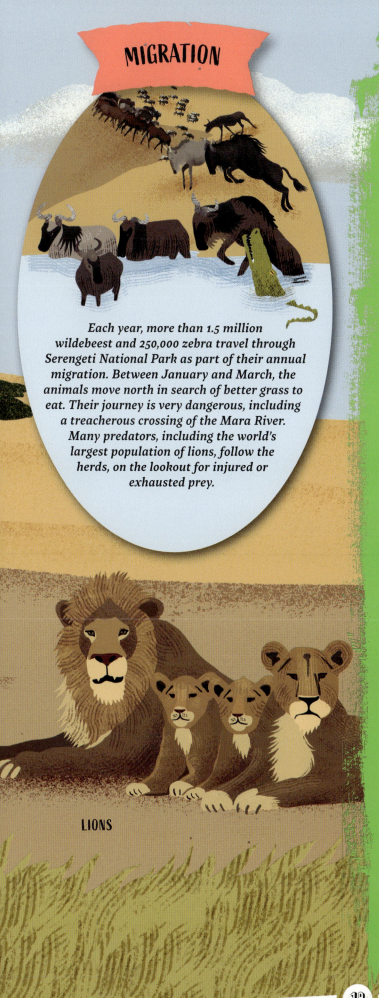

Each year, more than 1.5 million wildebeest and 250,000 zebra travel through Serengeti National Park as part of their annual migration. Between January and March, the animals move north in search of better grass to eat. Their journey is very dangerous, including a treacherous crossing of the Mara River. Many predators, including the world's largest population of lions, follow the herds, on the lookout for injured or exhausted prey.

LIONS

ACTIVITY

Lion head

Make a lion's head and mane.

1. Paint a paper plate yellow. With help from an adult, cut strips of brown, orange, and yellow paper for the mane.

2. You'll need an adult to help you with the gluing in this activity. Run a glue stick around the rim of the back of the plate and stick on alternating yellow and orange strips, with a small gap between them. Glue the brown strips overlapping between the yellow and orange strips.

3. To make the ears, cut out two rounded pieces of yellow paper and two smaller rounded pieces of brown paper. Glue the brown pieces to the center of the yellow pieces and glue the ears in place, as shown.

4. To make the nose, cut out a triangular piece of brown paper and glue it to the center of the plate.

5. Finish off your lion's face by drawing on the mouth and whiskers and gluing two large googly eyes in place.

SOUTHERN AFRICA

Much of southern Africa is covered in high grasslands where many large animals are found. To the west is the Namib Desert, one of the harshest habitats in the world. Located 250 miles (400 km) off the east coast of Africa is the large island of Madagascar. More than 90 percent of Madagascar's plants and animals are unique to the island.

SKELETON COAST

Known to the local San people (see page 28) as "the Land God Made in Anger," the Skeleton Coast runs along the edge of the Namib Desert in southwest Africa. More than 1,000 ships have been wrecked attempting to navigate this part of the Atlantic Ocean. The coast is often covered in a thick fog, while strong winds whip up treacherous waves. For any ship's crew stranded on the beach, the only way out is across the desert, one of the driest places on Earth.

ELEPHANTS

Weighing up to 6 tons (5.4 mt), African elephants are the world's largest land animals. An elephant's tusks are elongated teeth. It uses its tusks to dig, lift objects, or strip bark from trees to eat. An elephant's trunk is an elongated nose that it uses for smelling, drinking, and grabbing hold of objects. Elephants live in tight-knit family groups and often twist their trunks with one another as a sign of affection.

THE HIGHVELD

The Highveld is a plateau in South Africa. It covers 154,440 square miles (400,000 sq km) of flat land that is about 4,900 feet (1,500 m) above sea level. Much of the Highveld has been turned into farmland, but the original grassland habitat has been preserved in a number of nature reserves. These are home to herds of mountain zebra; South Africa's national bird, the ground-dwelling blue crane; and Africa's largest snake, the African rock python, which can grow more than 20 feet (6 m) long.

MADAGASCAR

Madagascar is a large island in the Indian Ocean. Located about 250 miles (400 km) off the east coast of Africa, the island is home to a huge array of wildlife that is found nowhere else in the world. It features a wide range of habitats, including rainforests, mountains, and grasslands.

RING-TAILED LEMUR

LEMURS

Lemurs are tree-living primates found only on Madagascar. They range in weight from 20 pounds (9 kg) to just 1 ounce (28 g). Many lemurs have special adaptations to help them find food. The weird-looking aye-aye has an extra-long, thin middle finger. It taps the bark of trees in search of hidden grubs. When it finds a grub, it gnaws a hole in the bark with its teeth, then uses its long finger to pull the grub out.

FACTS

MADAGASCAR

- Madagascar is home to nearly half of the world's chameleons, including the tiny nano-chameleon, whose body is only 0.5 inch (13 mm) long — small enough to fit on a fingernail!

- Grandidier's baobab is a large tree with a long, cylindrical trunk up to 10 feet (3 m) across. It uses its massive trunk to store water to help it survive droughts.

PANTHER CHAMELEON

SATANIC LEAF-TAILED GECKO

GRANDIDIER'S BAOBAB

FOSSA

HISSING COCKROACH

ACTIVITY

Build a baobab

Make a cardboard baobab tree.

1. Use a black crayon to draw lines around a brown cardboard tube to represent the bark of the tree's trunk. You can use a short cardboard tube or a long one to make a really tall tree.

2. With adult help, use scissors to cut slits about 1 inch (2.5 cm) long around one end of the tube. Pull back the tabs so that they fan out. These are the branches of your tree.

3. Tape a small piece of green paper to the tip of each branch to represent the leaves.

OKAVANGO DELTA

The Okavango Delta is a grassy plain in Botswana in southern Africa. Each year, the delta floods with water from the Okavango River, creating lakes, canals, and swamps. The plentiful fresh water attracts animals of all kinds from far and wide.

FACTS

- Cheetahs are the world's fastest land animals. They can reach speeds of up to 60 miles (100 km) per hour in short sprints.

- The southern white rhino is the second-largest land animal in the world, after the elephant. When threatened, it will attack using its huge horn.

AFRICAN FISH EAGLE

SPRINGBOKS

Springboks are antelopes with a spring in their step. They are hunted by many predators, including cheetahs, lions, and leopards. To escape capture, a springbok can run at more than 50 miles (80 km) per hour. When they are nervous, springboks are often seen stotting, or repeatedly leaping, 6.5 feet (2 m) into the air. It is thought that they do this to show potential predators that they are fit and healthy, and that easier prey lies elsewhere.

LIONS

HANDS-ON

Make a rainstick

A rainstick is an instrument played in Africa and elsewhere. Make one of your own.

1. Start by painting a long cardboard tube to make it look like wood. A tube from a roll of aluminum foil works well.

2. With help from an adult, cut out two circles from a paper bag. Secure one of the circles around one end of the tube with an elastic band.

3. Fill your rainstick with dry rice or beans. Use an elastic band to secure the open end of the tube with the second circle of paper. Decorate your rainstick by tying colored thread around it.

4. Explore the sounds your rainstick makes. Experiment with different combinations of filling to find your favorite sound.

GREAT MOSQUE OF DJENNÉ

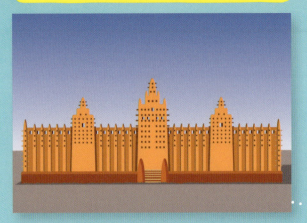

The Great Mosque of Djenné in Mali is the world's largest mud-brick building. Each April, the people of Djenné celebrate a festival in which they come together to plaster new mud to the mosque's walls. This is essential to allow the building to survive Mali's rainy season. The current mosque was built in 1907 on the site of an older mosque that was built 800 years ago, when Djenné became a center of Islamic scholarship in Africa.

PEOPLE AND PLACES

Human beings originate from Africa, and today the continent boasts the most diverse people and cultures of any continent. It is home to 1.3 billion people. North Africa generally refers to the countries to the north of the Sahara Desert, from Morocco in the west to Egypt in the east. These countries have predominantly Muslim, Arabic-speaking people. Sub-Saharan Africa refers to the countries to the south of the Sahara, where Christianity is often the dominant religion.

NIGERIA

Nigeria has the largest population of any country in Africa. In addition to the official language of English, hundreds of other languages are spoken. The largest city in Nigeria is Lagos. This bustling port city on the Gulf of Guinea is home to more than 10 million people. Lagos was replaced as Nigeria's capital in 1991 by Abuja, a brand-new city built inland on the green Chikuku Hills.

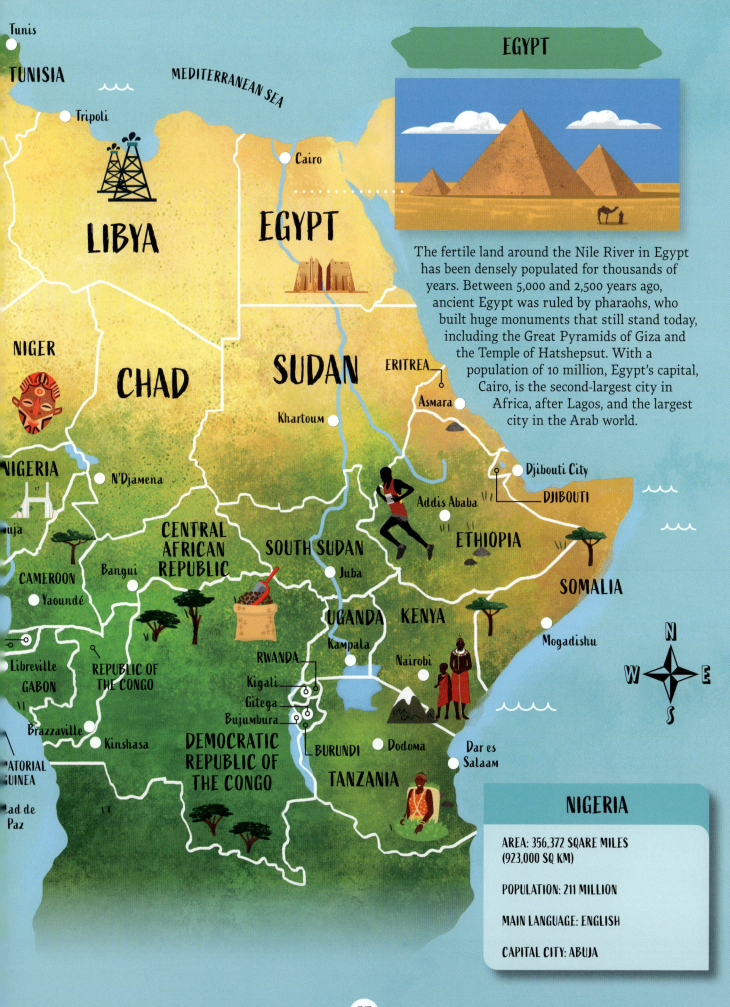

PEOPLE AND PLACES

Southern Africa is made up of eleven different countries. The people of southern Africa mostly speak languages belonging to one of two groups: Bantu or Xhosa. Europeans first arrived in the region in the seventeenth century, and today there are significant populations with European origins in South Africa, Zimbabwe, and Namibia.

THE SAN

The San are first nation people of southern Africa, which means that they are descended from the first human inhabitants of the area more than 100,000 years ago. The San are highly skilled and knowledgeable hunter-gatherers. The women gather fruit, vegetables, and insects and have a detailed knowledge of the uses of thousands of different plants. The men hunt animals using arrows and spears. They are expert trackers, capable of following a wounded animal for several days.

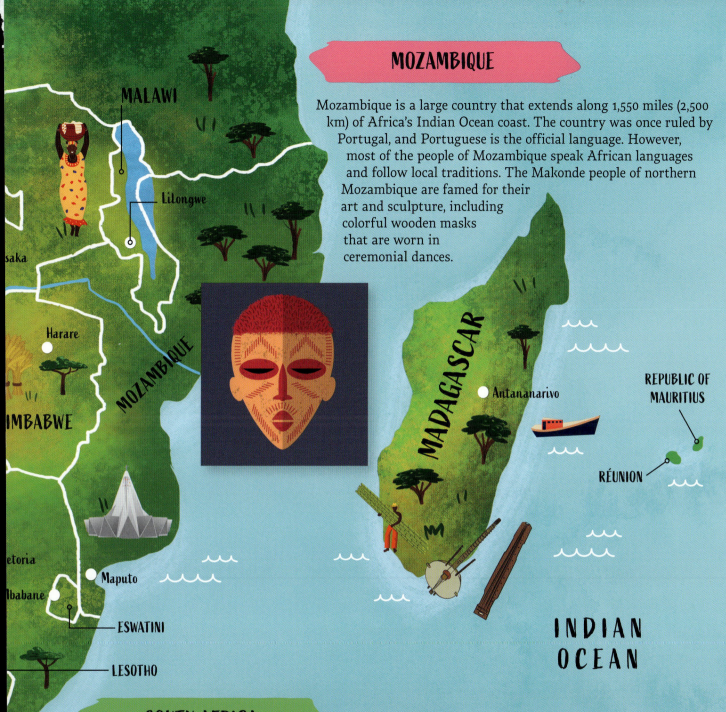

MOZAMBIQUE

Mozambique is a large country that extends along 1,550 miles (2,500 km) of Africa's Indian Ocean coast. The country was once ruled by Portugal, and Portuguese is the official language. However, most of the people of Mozambique speak African languages and follow local traditions. The Makonde people of northern Mozambique are famed for their art and sculpture, including colorful wooden masks that are worn in ceremonial dances.

SOUTH AFRICA

Known as the "Rainbow Nation," South Africa has a multicultural population that reflects its turbulent history. Once ruled by a white minority of European descent, South Africa is now a democracy. The design of the flag of South Africa includes elements of the flags of the South African Republic and the African National Congress.

SOUTH AFRICA

AREA: 436,322 SQUARE MILES (1.2 MILLION SQ KM)

POPULATION: 60 MILLION

MAIN LANGUAGES: 11 OFFICIAL LANGUAGES, INCLUDING ZULU, XHOSA, AFRIKAANS, AND ENGLISH

CAPITAL CITIES: PRETORIA, BLOEMFONTEIN, AND CAPE TOWN

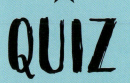

QUIZ

1. What is the name of the narrow strip of water that separates Africa from Europe?

2. What is the name for the dominant males that lead family groups of mountain gorillas?

3. The Maasai make a traditional drink by mixing cow's milk with which other liquid?

4. The Skeleton Coast runs along the edge of which desert?

5. What is the name of Africa's largest snake?

6. Which tree-living primates are found only on Madagascar?

7. What does the Grandidier's baobab tree store in its trunk to help it survive droughts?

8. What is the largest land animal in the world?

9. The Great Mosque of Djenné is found in which country?

10. What is the largest city in Africa?

11. Mozambique was once ruled by which European country?

12. What are the three capital cities of South Africa?

Answers:
1. Strait of Gibraltar 2. silverbacks 3. cow's blood 4. Namib Desert 5. African rock python 6. Lemurs 7. Water 8. African elephant 9. Mali 10. Lagos 11. Portugal 12. Pretoria, Bloemfontein, and Cape Town

GLOSSARY

Delta
A flat, fan-shaped area of land created where a river splits into many different branches.

Dormant
Relates to a volcano that has erupted in the past but is not likely to erupt any time soon.

Drought
A period of time where little or no rain falls, leading to a water shortage.

Elongated
Something that has been stretched out.

Equator
An imaginary line around Earth that is the same distance from both the North and South Poles. The equator divides the planet into the Northern Hemisphere and the Southern Hemisphere.

Famine
A period when very little food is available.

Fertile
Relating to soil that can grow a lot of crops.

Great apes
A group of tailless primates that includes chimpanzees, gorillas, orangutans, and humans.

Habitat
An area with the right conditions for a particular set of plants, animals, and other living things to live. Those conditions may include soil type, rainfall, or temperature.

Migration
The movement of animals and people from one place to another.

Moorland
Open upland areas of land where grasses, bushes, and heather grow.

Nature reserve
A specific area where wildlife is protected.

Oasis
(Plural: oases) A fertile area in a desert where water near the surface allows plants to grow.

Plateau
(Plural: plateaus) An area of high, flat ground.

Predator
An animal that hunts and eats other animals.

Primates
A group of mammals that includes monkeys, apes, and lemurs. Primates have hands with which they can manipulate objects.

Rainforest
A dense forest rich in life that grows in areas with plentiful rainfall all year round.

Species
A group of closely related living things that reproduce with one another.

Swamp
An area of wetland that is partially covered in water or is flooded with water at certain times of the year.

INDEX

antelopes 11, 25
area of Africa 5
Aswan High Dam 7
Atlas Mountains 6
aye-ayes 22

baboons 16
baobabs 22, 23
bonobos 13

camels 6
Central Africa 10–19
chameleons 22
cheetahs 24
cichlids 14
cloud forests 11
Congo Rainforest 12–13
crocodiles 18

deserts 5, 6, 8–9, 20

Egypt 7, 27
elephants 21
Ethiopian Highlands 11

farming 7
fennec foxes 8

Grand Erg 8
grasslands 5, 18, 20
Great Mosque of Djenné 26
groundsels 16

habitats 5
Highveld 21

hippos 14
hornbills 16

ibex 11
Islam 8, 26

Lake Victoria 14
languages 26, 28, 29
lemurs 22
leopards 18
lions 19
location of Africa 4
lungfish 12

Maasai people 14, 15
Madagascar 20, 22–23
Makonde people 29
Mali 8, 26
maps, political and
    physical 5
Mount Kilimanjaro 16–17
mountain gorillas 11
mountains 5, 6, 16–17
Mozambique 29

Namib Desert 20
Nigeria 26, 27
Nile River 6, 7
nomadic people 7
northern Africa 6–9, 26

Okavango Delta 24–25

parrots 12, 13
pythons 21

rainfall 10
rainforests 5, 12–13
rainsticks 25
religions 26
rhinos 24
Rift Valley Lakes 14–15
rivers 5, 6, 7, 12
Roof of Africa 11

Sahara Desert 6, 7, 8–9
Sahel 7
San Antonio de Ureka 10
San people 20, 28
sand dunes 8, 9
Serengeti National Park
    18–19
Skeleton Coast 20
South Africa 21, 29
southern Africa 20–21,
    28–29
springboks 25
sub-Saharan Africa 26

Timbuktu 8
turtles 10

volcanoes 17

wildebeest 18, 19
wolves 11

zebra 18, 19, 21